Playi

Jane Austens

Pride & Prejudice
FOR KIDS
(The melodramatic version!)

For 8-16+ actors, or kids of all ages who want to have fun!
Creatively modified by
Khara C. Barnhart and Brendan P. Kelso
Cover illustrations by Shana Hallmeyer, Adam Watson,
Ryan Gottlieb, and Ron Leishman
Special Contributor: Asif Zamir

3 Melodramatic Modifications of Jane Austen's Novel
for 3 different group sizes:

8-10+ actors

11-13+ actors

14-16+ actors

Table Of Contents

For Cecilia, my wondrous fourth and final act.
-KCB

To Rosie, who has brought so much joy into our lives.
-BPK

Foreword

When I was in high school there was something about Shakespeare that appealed to me. Not that I understood it mind you, but there were clear scenes and images that always stood out in my mind. Romeo & Juliet, "Romeo, Romeo; wherefore art thou Romeo?"; Julius Caesar, "Et tu Brute"; Macbeth, "Double, Double, toil and trouble"; Hamlet, "to be or not to be"; A Midsummer Night's Dream, all I remember about this was a wickedly cool fairy and something about a guy turning into a donkey that I thought was pretty funny. It was not until I started analyzing Shakespeare's plays as an actor that I realized one very important thing, I still didn't understand them. Seriously though, it's tough enough for adults, let alone kids. Then it hit me, why don't I make a version that kids could perform, but make it easy for them to understand with a splash of Shakespeare lingo mixed in? And voila! A melodramatic masterpiece was created! They are intended to be melodramatically fun!

THE PLAYS: There are 3 plays within this book, for three different group sizes. The reason: to allow educators or parents to get the story across to their children regardless of the size of their group. As you read through the plays, there are several lines that are highlighted. These are actual lines from the original book. I am a little more particular about the kids saying these lines verbatim. But the rest, well... have fun!

The entire purpose of this book is to instill the love of a classic story, as well as drama, into the kids.

And when you have children who have a passion for something, they will start to teach themselves, with or without school.

These plays are intended for pure fun. Please DO NOT have the kids learn these lines verbatim, that would be a complete waste of creativity. But do have them basically know their lines and improvise wherever they want as long as it pertains to telling the story. Because that is the goal of an actor: to tell the story. In A Midsummer Night's Dream, I once had a student playing Quince question me about one of her lines, "but in the actual story, didn't the Mechanicals state that 'they would hang us'?" I thought for a second and realized that she had read the story with her mom, and she was right. So I let her add the line she wanted and it added that much more fun, it made the play theirs. I have had kids throw water on the audience, run around the audience, sit in the audience, lose their pumpkin pants (size 30 around a size 15 doesn't work very well, but makes for some great humor!) and most importantly, die all over the stage. The kids love it.

One last note: if you want some educational resources, loved our plays, want to tell the world how much your kids loved performing Shakespeare, want to insult someone with our Shakespeare Insult Generator, or are just a fan of Shakespeare, then hop on our website and have fun:

PlayingWithPlays.com

With these notes, I'll see you on the stage, have fun, and break a leg!

SCHOOL, AFTERSCHOOL, and SUMMER classes

I've been teaching these plays as afterschool and summer programs for quite some time. Many people have asked what the program is, therefore, I have put together a basic formula so any teacher or parent can follow and have melodramatic success! As well, many teachers use my books in a variety of ways. You can view the formula and many more resources on my website at: PlayingWithPlays.com

ROYALTIES

I am asked all the time about royalties for my plays. So, here are the basic rules:

1) Please contact me! I always LOVE to hear about a school or group performing my books!

2) If you are a group and DO NOT charge your kids to be in this production: contact me, and we can talk about waiving the book costs or discounts on signed copies.

3) If you are a group and DO NOT charge the audience to see the plays, there is no royalty! (but, please leave a positive review, and send some photos!)

4) If you are a group and DO charge your kids to be in the production, contact me as I will give you a bulk discount (8 books or more), sign each book, and send some really cool press on Shakespeare tattoos!

5) If you are a group and DO charge the audience to see the performance, please contact me to discuss royalty options.

Any other questions or comments, please email me at:

contact@PlayingWithPlays.com

The 15-Minute or so Pride & Prejudice
By Jane Austen
Creatively modified by
Khara C. Barnhart & Brendan P. Kelso
8-10+ Actors

CAST OF CHARACTERS:

ELIZABETH BENNET: Witty and smart young lady

MR. DARCY: Proud young man, in love with Elizabeth

MR. BENNET: Elizabeth's father

MRS. BENNET: Elizabeth's mother

[1]**JANE BENNET:** Elizabeth's older sister, loves Mr. Bingley

MARY/CATHERINE (KITTY)/LYDIA BENNET: Elizabeth's younger sisters (one enthusiastic actor)

[1]**CHARLOTTE LUCAS:** Elizabeth's best friend

[2]**CHARLES BINGLEY:** Rich and good, in love with Jane

GEORGE WICKHAM: A charming officer, runs off with Lydia

[2]**MR. COLLINS:** Elizabeth's boring cousin; marries Charlotte

[1]JANE BENNET and CHARLOTTE LUCAS can be played by the same actor

[2]CHARLES BINGLEY and MR. COLLINS can be played by the same actor

ACT 1 SCENE 1

(Enter ELIZABETH)

ELIZABETH: *(to audience)* It is a truth universally acknowledged, that a single man in possession of a good fortune, must be in want of a wife. Am I right?

(enter MR. and MRS. BENNET)

MRS. BENNET: Guess what, Mr. Bennet! A rich, single man named Mr. Bingley is moving into the neighborhood! What a fine thing for our girls!

MR. BENNET: Mrs. Bennet, how so?

MRS. BENNET: So he can marry one of them, of course!

ELIZABETH: *(to audience)* My mom wastes no time. *(to MR. and MRS. BENNET)* Hey, maybe he'll be at the ball next week!

MRS. BENNET: Oh, Elizabeth, of course, the ball! *(calls offstage)* Girls!

(enter JANE and MARY/KITTY/LYDIA, running and jumping with excitement)

ELIZABETH: *(to audience)* My sisters...wait. Why are there only two of you? There's supposed to be four of you!

MARY/KITTY/LYDIA: Well, you know. Not enough actors. So I'm Mary, Kitty, AND Lydia.

JANE: And I'm just Jane.

MRS. BENNET: Oh whatever, let's get to the ball!

ALL GIRLS: *(squealing)* To the ball! *(ALL characters onstage spin around and strike a pose)*

(enter MR. BINGLEY and MR. DARCY; ALL characters who are not speaking are dancing silently onstage except for MR. DARCY, who stands still center stage)

MR. BINGLEY: *(to JANE)* Hi! I'm Charles Bingley. I'm really rich. I also have a great sense of humor.

JANE: Hi, I'm Jane. I think I like you. *(they begin dancing together)*

MARY/KITTY/LYDIA: Who's the other guy?

ELIZABETH: That's Mr. Darcy. I heard he's the proudest, most disagreeable man in the world.

MR. DARCY: *(looking around the room and speaking to himself)* Ugh. Boring. I detest dancing. Plus, there is not a woman in the room whom it would not be a punishment to dance with.

MR. BINGLEY: *(to MR. DARCY)* What about her? *(he points to ELIZABETH; ELIZABETH waves)*

MR. DARCY: She is tolerable, but not handsome enough to tempt ME.

ELIZABETH: Wow. Ouch.

JANE: Oh don't listen to him, Elizabeth. He's a meanie.

ELIZABETH: Thanks, Jane. You're my favorite sister! Let's dance.

(ALL exit, still dancing; MR. DARCY exits last, not smiling or dancing)

(enter ELIZABETH, MARY/KITTY/LYDIA, MR. BENNET and MRS. BENNET)

MRS. BENNET: Well, girls, we certainly have had a lot of fun lately at all these dances.

MARY/KITTY/LYDIA: And how strange, Lizzy, that Mr. Darcy keeps trying to dance with you after he insulted you. Maybe he likes you now!

(MR. DARCY pops his head onstage)

MR. DARCY: *(to audience)* It's true. *(melodramatic sigh)* I'm reluctantly forced to acknowledge her figure to be light and pleasing, and I am caught by her easy playfulness. In other words, Elizabeth Bennet is pretty and fun. Ugh! *(he returns offstage)*

ELIZABETH: Well I could never like him. And I'll never dance with him, so there!

MARY/KITTY/LYDIA: Can we please talk about something more interesting? Like, the officers?! They're SO handsome and SO brave! *(she squeals)*

MR. BENNET: From all that I can collect by your manner of talking, you must be...the silliest girls in the country. I have suspected it some time, but I am now convinced.

(enter JANE)

JANE: Guess what! I've been invited to Mr. Bingley's house for a visit!

MARY/KITTY/LYDIA: Ooooooo! He likes youuuuuuuuu!

MRS. BENNET: Better go on horseback, because it seems likely to rain; and then you must stay all night.

ELIZABETH: *(sarcastically)* Really? Solid plan, Mom.

JANE: Okay, bye! *(she exits)*

MARY/KITTY/LYDIA: Hey, look, it's raining!

MRS. BENNET: Woot! My plan is working! *(starts dancing around in a victory dance; ALL exit)*

(enter JANE, MR. BINGLEY, MR. DARCY, and ELIZABETH; JANE lies on the floor upstage; MR. DARCY is ignoring everyone while reading a book; ELIZABETH enters opposite the rest)

ELIZABETH: Howdy. I'm just here to check on Jane since she got sick from the rain. Hey, that rhymed!

MR. BINGLEY: Welcome! I'm so sorry she got sick. *(JANE coughs in the background)* Want to walk with me? *(holds out his arm to ELIZABETH)*

ELIZABETH: Um, walk where?

MR. BINGLEY: You know, take a turn about the room. *(to audience)* This is what people did before television.

(MR. BINGLEY and ELIZABETH walk in a large circle around MR. DARCY)

MR. BINGLEY: *(calls over to JANE)* How ya doing, Jane?

(JANE, still lying on the floor, gives two thumbs up and coughs some more)

MR. BINGLEY: *(to ELIZABETH)* What do you think of Mr. Darcy?

ELIZABETH: Are we talking strengths or weaknesses? Because he doesn't seem like a warm, fuzzy, or forgiving person.

MR. DARCY: My good opinion once lost, is lost forever.

ELIZABETH: *(to MR. BINGLEY)* See? *(to MR. DARCY)* So your defect is to hate everybody.

MR. DARCY: And yours is to willfully misunderstand them. *(JANE moans)*

ELIZABETH: Whatever. I really don't have time for this. Peace out. *(she walks over to JANE and drags her offstage)*

(ALL exit)

ACT 1 SCENE 4

(enter ALL BENNETS and MR. COLLINS)

MR. BENNET: Girls, meet my cousin, Mr. Collins, who, when I am dead, may turn you all out of this house as soon as he pleases.

ELIZABETH: Wait a minute. Just because we're GIRLS, we can't inherit the house or property?

MARY/KITTY/LYDIA: That's soooooo dumb. *(to audience)* No wonder we're all so focused on getting married.

MR. COLLINS: Stinks to be you. Don't worry; I'll take good care of this house someday.

JANE: Let's go to town. You know, get some fresh air. *(MR. and MRS. BENNET exit; ALL others begin walking around the stage in large circle; enter MR. WICKHAM)*

MARY/KITTY/LYDIA: An officer! An officer!

ELIZABETH: *(to MR. WICKHAM)* Hi!

WICKHAM: Hello, ladies! My name is Wickham. I am very handsome and very charming. So you should TOTALLY believe everything I say. *(strikes a pose)*

ELIZABETH: Makes sense.

JANE and MARY/KITTY/LYDIA: *(to audience, using "jazz hands")* Foreshadowing!

(enter MR. DARCY on a hobby horse, trotting towards the group onstage. He stops in front of MR. WICKHAM and looks disgusted)

MR. DARCY: *(to MR. WICKHAM)* Ugh.

WICKHAM: Ugh to you too. *(sticks out tongue at MR. DARCY and makes spitting noises; MR. DARCY does the same to WICKHAM; MR. DARCY "rides" offstage in a huff)*

ELIZABETH: Um, what was that about?

(MR. WICKHAM takes ELIZABETH's arm and leads her away from the other characters. ALL others whisper amongst themselves)

WICKHAM: Let me tell you my super sad story. That guy on the horse, Mr. Darcy? Well, his dad was my godfather and was going to give me some money so I could be a minister. Then when his dad died, Mr. Darcy didn't give me any money! And I was forced to be a soldier! And Mr. Darcy hates me! *(starts crying melodramatically)*

ELIZABETH: This is quite shocking! He deserves to be publically disgraced! I had not thought Mr. Darcy so bad as this...though I have never liked him.

MR. COLLINS: This town smells like horse poop. Let's leave.

ELIZABETH: *(to MR. WICKHAM)* Gotta go, Mr. Wickham. See ya.

WICKHAM: See ya. *(he bows extravagantly)*

(ALL exit)

ACT 1 SCENE 5

(enter ELIZABETH)

ELIZABETH: *(to audience)* You'll never guess where we are now. That's right. Another dance! I was hoping that cute Mr. Wickham would be here, but no luck. I've had to dance with my boring cousin, Mr. Collins, and that terrible Mr. Darcy. *(MR. COLLINS and MR. DARCY enter from opposite sides of the stage and strike dance poses)* Meanwhile, my sister Jane seems to be happily in love with Mr. Bingley. *(enter JANE, who begins dancing around the stage, looking super happy)*

(MR. COLLINS walks over to ELIZABETH; MR. DARCY and JANE exit)

MR. COLLINS: So, Elizabeth, I've decided I need a wife. As soon as I saw you, I singled you out as the companion of my future life. Let's get married!

ELIZABETH: What? No way!

(enter MRS. BENNET, running)

MRS. BENNET: Whaaaaaaaat?? Lizzy, you marry him right now!

ELIZABETH: Um, yeah. Not happening, mom.

MRS. BENNET: *(calls offstage)* Mr. Bennet!! *(enter MR. BENNET)* Make Elizabeth marry Mr. Collins!

MR. BENNET: *(looks at MR. COLLINS, then ELIZABETH, then MRS. BENNET; sighs loudly)* Elizabeth, from this day you must be a stranger to one of your parents. Your mother will never see you again if you do NOT marry Mr. Collins, and I will never see you again if you DO.

MRS. BENNET: Whaaaaaaaat? But...

ELIZABETH: Thanks for having my back, Dad! *(to MR. COLLINS and MRS. BENNET)* Can we forget this whole conversation now?

(enter CHARLOTTE LUCAS)

CHARLOTTE: *(to ELIZABETH)* Hey there, my best friend!!

ELIZABETH: Hey Charlotte!

MR. COLLINS: *(interrupting)* Charlotte...you look like you have...uhhhh...a nice personality.

CHARLOTTE: Thanks!

MR. COLLINS: *(pushes ELIZABETH behind him)* Will YOU marry me?

CHARLOTTE: *(to audience)* He's neither sensible, nor agreeable, but... *(to MR. COLLINS)* Sure, why not?

MR. COLLINS: Perfect. *(to the BENNETS)* Later! *(he and CHARLOTTE link arms and exit)*

MRS. BENNET: See, now there's a girl with some sense.

(ALL exit)

ACT 2 SCENE 1

(enter ELIZABETH and JANE; JANE holds a letter)

JANE: They're gone, Lizzy, all gone! Mr. Bingley and Mr. Darcy have left town and they're not coming back.

ELIZABETH: Good riddance.

JANE: How can you say that! I thought Mr. Bingley was going to marry me. But in this letter, his sister basically says that he's going to marry Mr. Darcy's sister, Georgiana!

ELIZABETH: Look, Jane, Mr. Bingley's sister is a brat. She thinks we have no money and sees that her brother is in love with you, and wants him to marry Georgiana. Well, I KNOW he loves you. Don't worry. Be happy.

JANE: No! He will be forgot, and we shall all be as we were before... single!

ELIZABETH: How depressing. But okay, if you say so.

JANE: And also, I hope you're not thinking of falling in love with Mr. Wickham. You must not let your fancy run away with you. He's not good enough for you. Okay, well, I'm going to go visit our aunt and uncle in London. Bye!

ELIZABETH: Bye! *(to audience)* At present, I am not in love with Mr. Wickham. But he is, beyond all comparison, the most agreeable man I ever saw. *(she sighs; MARY/KITTY/LYDIA runs onstage and whispers in ELIZABETH'S ear, then runs offstage)* Oh. Well, apparently Mr. Wickham likes someone else now. Some rich girl. I guess handsome young men must have something to live on as well as the plain. You know, I should really go visit my best friend Charlotte and see if she likes being married to boring Mr. Collins.

ACT 2 SCENE 2

(ELIZABETH starts walking around the stage. Enter CHARLOTTE and MR. COLLINS)

MR. COLLINS: Welcome, Elizabeth.

CHARLOTTE: You came! I'm a wife now!

ELIZABETH: I know! How weird!

(enter MR. DARCY; CHARLOTTE and MR. COLLINS tiptoe offstage)

ELIZABETH: What are YOU doing here?

MR. DARCY: Visiting my aunt. She lives right over there. *(he points in a random direction)* What are YOU doing here?

ELIZABETH: Visiting my best friend. *(motions to where CHARLOTTE was standing and notices that she is now gone)*

MR. DARCY: *(to audience)* Okay. I'm going to skip ahead now because we can't possibly fit every conversation Jane Austen wrote into this play. So Elizabeth and I keep running into each other and each time I realize more and more how smart and amazing she is...

ELIZABETH: *(taps MR. DARCY on the shoulder)* Um, hello?

MR. DARCY: *(takes a deep breath)* In vain I have struggled. It will not do. My feelings will not be repressed. You must allow me to tell you how ardently I admire and love you. Will you marry me?

ELIZABETH: Are you kidding me?

MR. DARCY: Is that a yes?

ELIZABETH: Look. I know you didn't want Mr. Bingley to marry my sister, Jane, because we're poor and my mom's kind of annoying. And I know how terrible you were to Mr. Wickham, leaving him with no money. Why would I marry you? I mean, come on.

MR. DARCY: So...is that a yes?

ELIZABETH: You are the last man in the world whom I could ever be prevailed on to marry. So...no!

MR. DARCY: Fine. *(throws a letter at her)* Read this when you're ready. *(he exits)*

(ELIZABETH picks letter up off floor, rolls her eyes at the audience, and exits)

(enter ELIZABETH)

ELIZABETH: *(to audience)* So, of course, I read his letter. He said that he DID give money to Mr. Wickham after his dad died, but Mr. Wickham spent all the money and then tried to elope with Mr. Darcy's younger sister, Georgiana, in order to get his hands on HER money! Say whaaaaaat? And I thought Mr. Wickham was such a gentleman! I was SO wrong! He's kind of a creep!

(enter JANE and MARY/KITTY/LYDIA)

MARY/KITTY/LYDIA: Welcome home! Guess what! We heard that the officers will be encamped near Brighton this summer. We want Dad to take us there! Because... officers!

ELIZABETH: Seriously? Can't you talk about anything else?

MARY/KITTY/LYDIA: Well what about you and Jane? Have you seen any pleasant men? Have you had any flirting? I mean, you both are going to be old maids soon. *(to ELIZABETH)* What, you're about 20 now, right?

JANE: You're so sweet, Lydia. Or Kitty. Or whoever you're being right now.

(enter MR. BENNET)

MR. BENNET: Lydia, the wife of some colonel has invited you to Brighton for the summer, so I guess you can go. *(to audience)* Hopefully, that colonel will keep her out of any real mischief.

JANE and ELIZABETH: *(to audience)* Foreshadowing! *(jazz hands)*

MARY/KITTY/LYDIA: Hurray! *(she exits)*

ELIZABETH: Okay, I need to get out of town. Maybe a trip to the countryside would be nice. Off I go in pursuit of novelty and amusement!

(ALL exit)

ACT 2 SCENE 4

(enter ELIZABETH)

ELIZABETH: *(looks around; to audience)* Wow, the countryside is great! Hey, look, a giant mansion! *(points across stage)* Oh, it's Pemberley! Because, of course, big houses deserve fancy sounding names. Also, this particular house belongs to Mr. Darcy. I really don't want to see him, so let's hope he's not home!

(she walks across the stage)

ELIZABETH: *(looking at the "house")* Oooooo! What an amazing house!

(enter MR. DARCY and MR. BINGLEY)

MR. DARCY: What are you doing here?

ELIZABETH: What are YOU doing here?

MR. DARCY: Ummm, this is my house.

ELIZABETH: Makes sense. *(to MR. BINGLEY)* Long time no see.

MR. BINGLEY: How's your sister, Jane?

ELIZABETH: She's... *(enter JANE)* here?!

JANE: *(to audience)* Shhhhhhh. I'm not really here. *(to ELIZABETH)* At this part in the story, I've sent you a bunch of letters, and well, here they are! *(hands ELIZABETH letters and runs offstage; ELIZABETH walks to a corner of the stage and starts reading the letters)*

MR. BINGLEY: You keep staring at Elizabeth.

MR. DARCY: Because I think she is one of the handsomest women of my acquaintance!

ELIZABETH: *(gasps)* OH NO! My sister Lydia has run off with Mr. Wickham! This is terrible! We have to go home right now!

MR. DARCY: That two-faced villain! Yes, you should hurry home now!

(ALL exit)

(enter MRS. BENNET, JANE, and ELIZABETH; they are ALL weeping and wailing)

MRS. BENNET: Poor dear child! And now here's Mr. Bennet gone away to look for her, and I know he will fight Wickham, and then he will be killed!

ELIZABETH: That might be a tad dramatic, Mom.

(enter MR. BENNET, running)

MR. BENNET: We found Lydia and Wickham. Here's the deal. Wickham says he'll marry her IF we pay him some money every year.

MRS. BENNET: He HAS to marry her or her honor will be ruined forever!

MR. BENNET: I know. I don't like it, but we have no choice!

(enter MARY/KITTY/LYDIA and MR. WICKHAM)

MARY/KITTY/LYDIA: I am a married woman! What about my sisters? *(to MRS. BENNET)* They must all go to Brighton. That is the place to get husbands. *(she and MR. WICKHAM laugh)*

ELIZABETH: Um, yeah, no thanks. I do not particularly like your way of getting husbands.

MARY/KITTY/LYDIA: Oh, and let me tell you about the wedding! Let's see. Our aunt and uncle were there, and Mr. Darcy, and... *(MR. WICKHAM covers LYDIA'S mouth to keep her from talking)*

WICKHAM: Okay, that's enough. We should probably leave and get on with our life together.

MARY/KITTY/LYDIA: You're SO right! Bye, family! *(MARY/KITTY/LYDIA and MR. WICKHAM exit)*

ELIZABETH: *(to audience)* Wait. Mr. Darcy was at their wedding?!

(MARY/KITTY/LYDIA pops back onstage)

MARY/KITTY/LYDIA: *(to ELIZABETH)* Mr. Darcy is the one who found us! And he gave Wickham a bunch of money to marry me. Romantic, right? But he didn't want you to know. I think he really, really likes you. Well, that's all I came to say. Bye! *(she exits)*

(enter MR. DARCY and MR. BINGLEY)

MR. BINGLEY: Jane! *(JANE steps forward)* I love you! And, um, I want to marry you!

JANE: Tis too much! I do not deserve it! I'm soooooo happy! *(JANE and MR. BINGLEY start dancing together around the stage)*

MRS. BENNET: Two girls down, three to go! *(ALL exit except ELIZABETH)*

ELIZABETH: *(to audience)* I am kinda jealous. And...I think that I actually love Mr. Darcy! Argh!

(enter MR. DARCY)

MR. DARCY: Hey.

ELIZABETH: Hey.

ELIZABETH and MR. DARCY: So I... *(talking over each other)*

MR. DARCY: *(clears throat)* If your feelings are still what they were last April, tell me so at once. MY affections and wishes are unchanged, but one word from you will silence me on this subject for ever.

ELIZABETH: So you still want to get married?

MR. DARCY: YES!

ELIZABETH: Me too! *(they high-five)*

(enter MR. BENNET, MRS. BENNET, and JANE)

MR. BENNET: *(to ELIZABETH)* Wait! Are you out of your senses? I thought you hated him?

JANE: Oh Lizzy, it cannot be! What is actually happening right now? I'm so confused.

ELIZABETH: *(Big deep breath)* I was wrong. He's actually... a good person. *(THE BENNETS all gasp and whisper amongst themselves)*

MR. DARCY: Yes. We were both prideful...and prejudiced.

MR. BENNET: Well then, congratulations!

MRS. BENNET: You'll be so rich!

ELIZABETH: *(to MRS. BENNET)* I think you mean happy, right?

MRS. BENNET: Ummm sure, that's what I meant.

MR. DARCY: I'm sure that's what she meant.

ELIZABETH: Okay, family, we've got some weddings to plan. Let's DO this! *(ALL exit)*

THE END

The 20-Minute or so Pride & Prejudice

By Jane Austen

Creatively modified by
Khara C. Barnhart & Brendan P. Kelso

11-13+ Actors

CAST OF CHARACTERS:

ELIZABETH BENNET: Witty and smart young lady

MR. DARCY: Proud young man, in love with Elizabeth

MR. BENNET: Elizabeth's father

MRS. BENNET: Elizabeth's mother

JANE BENNET: Elizabeth's older sister, loves Mr. Bingley

[1]**CATHERINE BENNET (KITTY):** Yet another sister of Elizabeth

LYDIA BENNET: You guessed it – another sister (the youngest one)

[1]**CHARLOTTE LUCAS:** Elizabeth's best friend

[2]**CHARLES BINGLEY:** Rich and good, in love with Jane

CAROLINE BINGLEY: Charles's not-so-nice sister

GEORGE WICKHAM: A charming officer, runs off with Lydia

[2]**MR. COLLINS:** Elizabeth's boring cousin; marries Charlotte

MRS. GARDINER: Elizabeth's aunt

[1]KITTY and CHARLOTTE LUCAS can be played by the same actor
[2]CHARLES BINGLEY and MR. COLLINS can be played by the same actor

ACT 1 SCENE 1

(Enter ELIZABETH)

ELIZABETH: *(to audience)* It is a truth universally acknowledged, that a single man in possession of a good fortune, must be in want of a wife. Am I right?

(enter MR. and MRS. BENNET)

MRS. BENNET: Guess what, Mr. Bennet! A rich, single man named Mr. Bingley is moving into the neighborhood! What a fine thing for our girls!

MR. BENNET: Mrs. Bennet, how so?

MRS. BENNET: So he can marry one of them, of course!

ELIZABETH: *(to audience)* My mom wastes no time. *(to MR. and MRS. BENNET)* Hey, maybe he'll be at the ball next week!

MRS. BENNET: Oh, Elizabeth, of course, the ball! *(calls offstage)* Girls!

(enter JANE, LYDIA, and KITTY, running and jumping with excitement)

ELIZABETH: *(to audience)* My sisters, Jane, Lydia, and Kitty. *(she points to each one in turn as she names them)* Wait. I have FOUR sisters and there are only THREE of you.

KITTY: Oh, Elizabeth! Well, there weren't enough actors, so we decided we didn't need a Mary.

LYDIA: Mary was the boring sister anyway.

ELIZABETH: Alrighty then.

ALL GIRLS: *(squealing)* To the ball! *(ALL characters onstage spin around and strike a pose)*

(enter MR. BINGLEY, CAROLINE, and MR. DARCY. ALL characters who are not speaking are dancing silently onstage except for MR. DARCY, who stands still center stage)

MR. BINGLEY: *(to JANE)* Hi! I'm Charles Bingley. I'm really rich. I also have a great sense of humor.

JANE: Hi, I'm Jane. I think I like you. *(they begin dancing together)*

LYDIA: *(to KITTY)* Who's the other guy?

KITTY: That's Mr. Darcy. I heard he's the proudest, most disagreeable man in the world.

MR. DARCY: *(looking around the room and speaking to himself)* Ugh. Boring. I detest dancing. Plus, there is not a woman in the room whom it would not be a punishment to dance with.

MR. BINGLEY: *(to MR. DARCY)* What about her? *(he points to ELIZABETH; ELIZABETH waves)*

MR. DARCY: She is tolerable, but not handsome enough to tempt ME.

ELIZABETH: Wow. Ouch.

JANE: Oh don't listen to him, Elizabeth. He's a meanie.

ELIZABETH: Thanks, Jane. You're my favorite sister! Let's dance.

(ALL exit, still dancing; MR. DARCY exits last, not smiling or dancing)

ACT 1 SCENE 2

(enter ELIZABETH, KITTY, LYDIA, MR. BENNET and MRS. BENNET)

MRS. BENNET: Well, girls, we certainly have had a lot of fun lately at all these dances.

KITTY: And how strange, Lizzy, that Mr. Darcy keeps trying to dance with you after he insulted you. Maybe he likes you now!

(MR. DARCY pops his head onstage)

MR. DARCY: *(to audience)* It's true. *(melodramatic sigh)* I'm reluctantly forced to acknowledge her figure to be light and pleasing, and I am caught by her easy playfulness. In other words, Elizabeth Bennet is pretty and fun. Ugh! *(he returns offstage)*

ELIZABETH: Well I could never like him. And I'll never dance with him, so there!

LYDIA: Can we please talk about something more interesting?

KITTY: Like, the officers!

LYDIA: Oh, the officers! *(KITTY and LYDIA squeal)*

KITTY: So handsome!

LYDIA: So brave! *(they squeal again)*

MR. BENNET: From all that I can collect by your manner of talking, you must be two of the silliest girls in the country. I have suspected it some time, but I am now convinced.

(enter JANE)

JANE: Guess what! I've been invited to Mr. Bingley's house for a visit!

BENNET SISTERS: Ooooooo! He likes youuuuuuuuu!

MRS. BENNET: Better go on horseback, because it seems likely to rain; and then you must stay all night.

ELIZABETH: *(sarcastically)* Really? Solid plan, Mom.

JANE: Okay, bye! *(she exits)*

LYDIA: Hey, look, it's raining!

MRS. BENNET: Woot! My plan is working! *(starts dancing around in a victory dance; ALL exit)*

(enter JANE, MR. BINGLEY, CAROLINE, MR. DARCY, and ELIZABETH; JANE lies on the floor upstage; MR. DARCY is ignoring everyone while reading a book; ELIZABETH enters opposite the rest)

ELIZABETH: Howdy. I'm just here to check on Jane since she got sick from the rain. Hey, that rhymed!

MR. BINGLEY: Welcome! I'm so sorry she got sick. *(JANE coughs in the background)*

CAROLINE: Come walk with me. *(holds out her arm to ELIZABETH)*

ELIZABETH: Um, walk where, Caroline?

CAROLINE: You know, take a turn about the room. *(to audience)* This is what people did before television.

(CAROLINE and ELIZABETH walk in a large circle around MR. BINGLEY and MR. DARCY)

MR. DARCY: You girls are either walking because you have secret affairs to discuss, or because you want to be admired.

MR. BINGLEY: I think they look nice. *(calls over to JANE)* How ya doing, Jane?

(JANE, still lying on the floor, gives two thumbs up and coughs some more)

CAROLINE: *(to ELIZABETH)* What do you think of our Mr. Darcy?

ELIZABETH: Are we talking strengths or weaknesses? Because he doesn't seem like a warm, fuzzy, or forgiving person.

MR. DARCY: My good opinion once lost, is lost forever.

ELIZABETH: *(to CAROLINE)* See? *(to MR. DARCY)* So your defect is to hate everybody.

MR. DARCY: And yours is to willfully misunderstand them. *(JANE moans)*

ELIZABETH: Whatever. I really don't have time for this. Peace out. *(she walks over to JANE and drags her offstage)*

(ALL exit)

ACT 1 SCENE 4

(enter ALL BENNETS and MR. COLLINS)

MR. BENNET: Girls, meet my cousin, Mr. Collins, who, when I am dead, may turn you all out of this house as soon as he pleases.

LYDIA: Wait a minute. Just because we're GIRLS, we can't inherit the house or property?

KITTY: That's soooooo dumb. *(to audience)* No wonder we're all so focused on getting married.

MR. COLLINS: Stinks to be you. Don't worry; I'll take good care of this house someday.

JANE: Let's go to town. You know, get some fresh air. *(MR. and MRS. BENNET exit; ALL others begin walking around the stage in large circle; enter MR. WICKHAM)*

LYDIA: An officer! An officer!

ELIZABETH: *(to MR. WICKHAM)* Hi!

WICKHAM: Hello, ladies! My name is Wickham. I am very handsome and very charming. So you should TOTALLY believe everything I say. *(strikes a pose)*

ELIZABETH: Makes sense.

BENNET SISTERS (EXCEPT ELIZABETH): *(to audience, using "jazz hands")* Foreshadowing!

(enter MR. DARCY on a hobby horse, trotting towards the group onstage. He stops in front of MR. WICKHAM and looks disgusted)

MR. DARCY: *(to MR. WICKHAM)* Ugh.

WICKHAM: Ugh to you too. *(sticks out tongue at MR. DARCY and makes spitting noises; MR. DARCY does the same to WICKHAM; MR. DARCY "rides" offstage in a huff)*

ELIZABETH: Um, what was that about?

(MR. WICKHAM takes ELIZABETH's arm and leads her away from the other characters. ALL others whisper amongst themselves)

WICKHAM: Let me tell you my super sad story. That guy on the horse, Mr. Darcy? Well, his dad was my godfather and was going to give me some money so I could be a minister. Then when his dad died, Mr. Darcy didn't give me any money! And I was forced to be a soldier! And Mr. Darcy hates me! *(starts crying melodramatically)*

ELIZABETH: This is quite shocking! He deserves to be publically disgraced! I had not thought Mr. Darcy so bad as this...though I have never liked him.

MR. COLLINS: This town smells like horse poop. Let's leave.

ELIZABETH: *(to MR. WICKHAM)* Gotta go. See ya.

WICKHAM: See ya. *(he bows extravagantly)*

(ALL exit)

(enter ELIZABETH)

ELIZABETH: *(to audience)* You'll never guess where we are now. That's right. Another dance! I was hoping that cute Mr. Wickham would be here, but no luck. I've had to dance with my boring cousin, Mr. Collins, and that terrible Mr. Darcy. *(MR. COLLINS and MR. DARCY enter from opposite sides of the stage and strike dance poses)* Meanwhile, my sister Jane seems to be happily in love with Mr. Bingley. *(enter JANE, who begins dancing around the stage, looking super happy; enter CAROLINE BINGLEY)*

CAROLINE: *(to ELIZABETH)* So, I hear you are quite delighted with George Wickham! WELL, let me just tell you, as a friend, that you totally shouldn't believe him. I don't know what he told you, but I'm here to tell you, that Mr. Darcy has always been remarkably kind to him.

ELIZABETH: Whatever. Believe what you want, but I believe Mr. Wickham. He's just sooooo charming.

CAROLINE: Whatever. Only trying to help. *(she flips her hair as she exits)*

(MR. COLLINS walks over to ELIZABETH; MR. DARCY and JANE exit)

MR. COLLINS: So, Elizabeth, I've decided I need a wife. As soon as I saw you, I singled you out as the companion of my future life. Let's get married!

ELIZABETH: What? No way!

(enter MRS. BENNET, running)

MRS. BENNET: Whaaaaaaaat?? Lizzy, you marry him right now!

ELIZABETH: Um, yeah. Not happening, mom.

MRS. BENNET: *(calls offstage)* Mr. Bennet!! *(enter MR. BENNET)* Make Elizabeth marry Mr. Collins!

MR. BENNET: *(looks at MR. COLLINS, then ELIZABETH, then MRS. BENNET; sighs loudly)* Elizabeth, from this day you must be a stranger to one of your parents. Your mother will never see you again if you do NOT marry Mr. Collins, and I will never see you again if you DO.

MRS. BENNET: Whaaaaaaaat? But...

ELIZABETH: Thanks for having my back, Dad! *(to MR. COLLINS and MRS. BENNET)* Can we forget this whole conversation now?

(enter CHARLOTTE LUCAS)

CHARLOTTE: *(to ELIZABETH)* Hey there, my best friend!

ELIZABETH: Hey Charlotte!

MR. COLLINS: *(interrupting)* Charlotte...you look like you have...uhhhh...a nice personality.

CHARLOTTE: Thanks!

MR. COLLINS: *(pushes ELIZABETH behind him)* Will YOU marry me?

CHARLOTTE: *(to audience)* He's neither sensible, nor agreeable, but... *(to MR. COLLINS)* Sure, why not?

MR. COLLINS: Perfect. *(to the BENNETS)* Later! *(he and CHARLOTTE link arms and exit)*

MRS. BENNET: See, now there's a girl with some sense.

(ALL exit)

ACT 2 SCENE 1

(enter ELIZABETH and JANE; JANE holds a letter)

JANE: They're gone, Lizzy, all gone! Caroline, Mr. Bingley, and Mr. Darcy have left town and they're not coming back.

ELIZABETH: Good riddance.

JANE: How can you say that! I thought Mr. Bingley was going to marry me. But in this letter, Caroline basically says that he's going to marry Mr. Darcy's sister, Georgiana!

ELIZABETH: Look, Jane, Caroline's a brat. She thinks we have no money and sees that her brother is in love with you, and wants him to marry Georgiana. Well, I KNOW he loves you. Don't worry. Be happy.

JANE: No! He will be forgot, and we shall all be as we were before...single!

ELIZABETH: How depressing. But okay, if you say so.

(enter MRS. GARDINER and all the BENNETS)

KITTY: Welcome, Aunt Gardiner!

ALL BENNETS: Hi!

MRS. GARDINER: Thanks, Kitty! Hi family! Since we're short on time, I'll get right to the point: Jane, you look sad. How about you come back to London with me when I leave? And you, Elizabeth, I've gotta warn you about that officer, Mr. Wickham. You must not let your fancy run away with you. He doesn't have any money, so you really can't marry him. Okay, bye!
(MRS. GARDINER exits with JANE; all BENNETS except ELIZABETH exit opposite side of stage)

ELIZABETH: *(to audience)* At present, I am not in love with Mr. Wickham. But he is, beyond all comparison, the most agreeable man I ever saw. *(she sighs; KITTY runs onstage and whispers in ELIZABETH'S ear, then runs offstage)* Oh. Well, apparently Mr. Wickham likes someone else now. Some rich girl. I guess handsome young men must have something to live on as well as the plain. You know, I should really go visit Charlotte and see if she likes being married to Mr. Collins.

ACT 2 SCENE 2

(ELIZABETH starts walking around the stage. Enter CHARLOTTE and MR. COLLINS)

MR. COLLINS: Welcome, Elizabeth.

CHARLOTTE: You came! I'm a wife now!

ELIZABETH: I know! How weird!

(enter MR. DARCY; CHARLOTTE and MR. COLLINS tiptoe offstage)

ELIZABETH: What are YOU doing here?

MR. DARCY: Visiting my aunt. She lives right over there. *(he points in a random direction)* What are YOU doing here?

ELIZABETH: Visiting my best friend. *(motions to where CHARLOTTE was standing and notices that she is now gone)*

MR. DARCY: *(to audience)* Okay. I'm going to skip ahead now because we can't possibly fit every conversation Jane Austen wrote into this play. So Elizabeth and I keep running into each other and each time I realize more and more how smart and amazing she is...

ELIZABETH: *(taps MR. DARCY on the shoulder)* Um, hello?

MR. DARCY: *(takes a deep breath)* In vain I have struggled. It will not do. My feelings will not be repressed. You must allow me to tell you how ardently I admire and love you. Will you marry me?

ELIZABETH: Are you kidding me?

MR. DARCY: Is that a yes?

ELIZABETH: Look. I know you didn't want Mr. Bingley to marry my sister, Jane, because we're poor and my mom's kind of annoying. And I know how terrible you were to Mr. Wickham, leaving him with no money. Why would I marry you? I mean, come on.

MR. DARCY: So...is that a yes?

ELIZABETH: You are the last man in the world whom I could ever be prevailed on to marry. So...no!

MR. DARCY: Fine. *(throws a letter at her)* Read this when you're ready. *(he exits)*

(ELIZABETH picks letter up off floor, rolls her eyes at the audience, and exits)

(enter ELIZABETH)

ELIZABETH: *(to audience)* So, of course, I read his letter. He said that he DID give money to Mr. Wickham after his dad died, but Mr. Wickham spent all the money and then tried to elope with Mr. Darcy's younger sister, Georgiana, in order to get his hands on her money! Say whaaaaaat? And I thought Mr. Wickham was such a gentleman! I was SO wrong! He's kind of a creep!

(enter JANE, LYDIA, and KITTY)

KITTY: Welcome home! Guess what! We heard that the officers will be encamped near Brighton this summer.

LYDIA: We want Dad to take us there! Because... officers!

ELIZABETH: Seriously, girls? Can you talk about anything else?

LYDIA: Well what about you and Jane? Have you seen any pleasant men? Have you had any flirting? I mean, you both are going to be old maids soon. *(to ELIZABETH)* What, you're about 20 now, right?

JANE: You're so sweet, Lydia.

(enter MR. BENNET)

MR. BENNET: Lydia, the wife of some colonel has invited you to Brighton for the summer, so I guess you can go. *(to audience)* Hopefully, that colonel will keep her out of any real mischief.

JANE, ELIZABETH, & KITTY: *(to audience)* Foreshadowing! *(jazz hands)*

KITTY: Not fair! I want to go, too!

LYDIA: Too bad, so sad. See ya! *(she exits)*

(enter MRS. GARDINER)

KITTY: Hi Aunt Gardiner!

MRS. GARDINER: *(to ELIZABETH)* Hello! Wanna go take a tour of the English countryside? *(to audience)* Basically, I just show up to take my nieces places. It's what I'm good at.

ELIZABETH: Sure. Let's go in pursuit of novelty and amusement!

(ALL exit)

ACT 2 SCENE 4

(enter ELIZABETH and MRS. GARDINER)

ELIZABETH: *(looks around)* Wow, the countryside is great!

MRS. GARDINER: Hey, look! *(points across stage)* That's Pemberley! We should go check it out.

ELIZABETH: Sure! Looking at mansions is a great way to feel insignificant! *(to audience)* Pemberley is the name of the mansion. Because, of course, big houses deserve fancy sounding names. Also, this particular house belongs to Mr. Darcy. So let's hope he's not home!

(they walk across the stage)

MRS. GARDINER and ELIZABETH: *(looking at the "house")* Oooooo! Ahhhhhh.

(enter MR. DARCY, MR. BINGLEY, and CAROLINE)

MR. DARCY: What are you doing here?

ELIZABETH: What are YOU doing here?

MR. DARCY: Ummm, this is my house.

ELIZABETH: Makes sense. *(to MR. BINGLEY and CAROLINE)* Long time no see.

MR. BINGLEY: How's your sister, Jane?

ELIZABETH: She's... *(enter JANE)* here?!

JANE: *(to audience)* Shhhhhhh. I'm not really here. *(to ELIZABETH)* At this part in the story, I've sent you a bunch of letters, and well, here they are! *(hands ELIZABETH letters and runs offstage; ELIZABETH and MRS. GARDINER walk to a corner of the stage and start reading the letters)*

CAROLINE: *(to MR. DARCY, pointing to ELIZABETH)* For my own part, I must confess I never could see any beauty in her.

MR. DARCY: Well I think she is one of the handsomest women of my acquaintance!

ELIZABETH: *(gasps)* OH NO! My sister Lydia has run off with Mr. Wickham! This is terrible! We have to go home right now!

MR. DARCY: That two-faced villain! Yes, you should hurry home now!

(ALL exit)

(enter ALL BENNETS, except LYDIA and MR. BENNET; they are ALL weeping and wailing)

MRS. BENNET: Poor dear child! And now here's Mr. Bennet gone away to look for her, and I know he will fight Wickham, and then he will be killed!

ELIZABETH: That might be a tad dramatic, Mom.

(enter MR. BENNET, running)

MR. BENNET: We found Lydia and Wickham. Here's the deal. Wickham says he'll marry her IF we pay him some money every year.

MRS. BENNET: He HAS to marry her or her honor will be ruined forever!

MR. BENNET: I know. I don't like it, but we have no choice!

(enter LYDIA and MR. WICKHAM)

LYDIA: I am a married woman! What about my sisters? *(to MRS. BENNET)* They must all go to Brighton. That is the place to get husbands. *(she and MR. WICKHAM laugh)*

ELIZABETH: Um, yeah, no thanks. I do not particularly like your way of getting husbands.

LYDIA: Oh, and let me tell you about the wedding! Let's see. Our aunt and uncle were there, and Mr. Darcy, and... *(MR. WICKHAM covers LYDIA'S mouth to keep her from talking)*

WICKHAM: Okay, that's enough. We should probably leave and get on with our life together.

LYDIA: You're SO right! Bye, family! *(LYDIA and MR. WICKHAM exit)*

ELIZABETH: *(to audience)* Wait. Mr. Darcy was at their wedding?!

(enter MRS. GARDINER)

MRS. GARDINER: *(to ELIZABETH)* Lizzy, Mr. Darcy is the one who found them! And he gave Wickham a bunch of money to marry Lydia. But he didn't want you to know. I think he really, really likes you. Well, that's all I came to say. Bye! *(she exits)*

(enter MR. DARCY and MR. BINGLEY)

MR. BINGLEY: Jane! *(JANE steps forward)* I love you! And, um, I want to marry you!

JANE: Tis too much! I do not deserve it! I'm soooooo happy! *(JANE and MR. BINGLEY start dancing together around the stage)*

MRS. BENNET: Two girls down, three to go! *(ALL exit except ELIZABETH)*

ELIZABETH: *(to audience)* I am kinda jealous. And...I think that I actually love Mr. Darcy! Argh!

(enter MR. DARCY)

MR. DARCY: Hey.

ELIZABETH: Hey.

ELIZABETH and MR. DARCY: So I... *(talking over each other)*

MR. DARCY: *(clears throat)* If your feelings are still what they were last April, tell me so at once. MY affections and wishes are unchanged, but one word from you will silence me on this subject for ever.

ELIZABETH: So you still want to get married?

MR. DARCY: YES!

ELIZABETH: Me too! *(they high-five)*

(enter MR. BENNET, MRS. BENNET, JANE, and KITTY)

MR. BENNET: *(to ELIZABETH)* Wait! Are you out of your senses? I thought you hated him?

JANE: Oh Lizzy, it cannot be! What is actually happening right now? I'm so confused.

ELIZABETH: *(Big deep breath)* I was wrong. He's actually... a good person. *(THE BENNETS all gasp and whisper amongst themselves)*

MR. DARCY: Yes. We were both prideful...and prejudiced.

MR. BENNET: Well then, congratulations!

MRS. BENNET: You'll be so rich!

ELIZABETH: *(to MRS. BENNET)* I think you mean happy, right?

MRS. BENNET: Ummm sure, that's what I meant.

MR. DARCY: I'm sure that's what she meant.

KITTY: Okay, family, we've got some weddings to plan. Let's DO this! *(ALL exit)*

THE END

The 25-Minute or so Pride & Prejudice

By Jane Austen

Creatively modified by

Khara C. Barnhart & Brendan P. Kelso

14-16+ Actors

CAST OF CHARACTERS:

ELIZABETH BENNET: Witty and smart young lady

MR. DARCY: Proud young man, in love with Elizabeth

MR. BENNET: Elizabeth's father

MRS. BENNET: Elizabeth's mother

JANE BENNET: Elizabeth's older sister, loves Mr. Bingley

[1]**MARY BENNET:** Another sister of Elizabeth

CATHERINE BENNET (KITTY): Yes, another sister!

LYDIA BENNET: You guessed it, another sister (the youngest one)

CHARLOTTE LUCAS: Elizabeth's best friend

CHARLES BINGLEY: Rich and good, in love with Jane

CAROLINE BINGLEY: Charles's not-so-nice sister

GEORGE WICKHAM: A charming officer, runs off with Lydia

[2]**MR. COLLINS:** Elizabeth's boring cousin; marries Charlotte

[2]**MR. GARDINER:** Mrs. Bennet's brother

MRS. GARDINER: Mr. Gardiner's wife

[1]**LADY CATHERINE de BOURGH:** Mr. Darcy's rich, snobby aunt

[1]MARY BENNET and LADY CATHERINE de BOURGH can be played by the same actor

[2]MR. COLLINS and MR. GARDINER can be played by the same actor

ACT 1 SCENE 1

(Enter ELIZABETH)

ELIZABETH: *(to audience)* It is a truth universally acknowledged, that a single man in possession of a good fortune, must be in want of a wife. Am I right?

(enter MR. and MRS. BENNET)

MRS. BENNET: Guess what, Mr. Bennet! A rich, single man named Mr. Bingley is moving into the neighborhood! What a fine thing for our girls!

MR. BENNET: Mrs. Bennet, how so?

MRS. BENNET: So he can marry one of them, of course!

ELIZABETH: *(to audience)* My mom wastes no time. *(to MR. and MRS. BENNET)* Hey, maybe he'll be at the ball next week!

MRS. BENNET: Oh, Elizabeth, of course, the ball! *(calls offstage)* Girls!

(enter JANE, MARY, KITTY, LYDIA, and CHARLOTTE, running and jumping with excitement)

ELIZABETH: *(to audience)* My sisters, Jane, Mary, Kitty, and Lydia...and my friend, Charlotte. *(she points to each one in turn as she names them)*

ALL GIRLS: *(to audience)* Hi! *(squealing)* To the ball! *(ALL characters onstage spin around and strike a pose)*

(enter MR. BINGLEY, CAROLINE, and MR. DARCY; ALL characters who are not speaking are dancing silently onstage except for MR. DARCY, who stands still center stage)

MR. BINGLEY: *(to JANE)* Hi! I'm Charles Bingley. I'm really rich. I also have a great sense of humor.

JANE: Hi, I'm Jane. I think I like you. *(they begin dancing together)*

LYDIA: *(to KITTY)* Who's the other guy?

KITTY: That's Mr. Darcy. I heard he's the proudest, most disagreeable man in the world.

MR. DARCY: *(looking around the room and speaking to himself)* Ugh. Boring. I detest dancing. Plus, there is not a woman in the room whom it would not be a punishment to dance with.

MR. BINGLEY: *(to MR. DARCY)* What about her? *(he points to ELIZABETH; ELIZABETH waves)*

MR. DARCY: She is tolerable, but not handsome enough to tempt ME.

ELIZABETH: Wow. Ouch.

CHARLOTTE: Oh don't listen to him, Elizabeth. He's a meanie.

ELIZABETH: Thanks, Charlotte. You're the best friend ever! Let's dance.

(ALL exit, still dancing; MR. DARCY exits last, not smiling or dancing)

ACT 1 SCENE 2

(enter ELIZABETH, MARY, KITTY, LYDIA, MR. BENNET and MRS. BENNET)

MRS. BENNET: Well, girls, we certainly have had a lot of fun lately at all these dances.

MARY: And how strange, Lizzy, that Mr. Darcy keeps trying to dance with you after he insulted you. Maybe he likes you now!

(MR. DARCY pops his head onstage)

MR. DARCY: *(to audience)* It's true. *(melodramatic sigh)* I'm reluctantly forced to acknowledge her figure to be light and pleasing, and I am caught by her easy playfulness. In other words, Elizabeth Bennet is pretty and fun. Ugh! *(he returns offstage)*

ELIZABETH: Well I could never like him. And I'll never dance with him, so there!

LYDIA: Can we please talk about something more interesting?

KITTY: Like, the officers!

LYDIA: Oh, the officers! *(KITTY and LYDIA squeal)*

KITTY: So handsome!

LYDIA: So brave! *(they squeal again)*

MR. BENNET: From all that I can collect by your manner of talking, you must be two of the silliest girls in the country. I have suspected it some time, but I am now convinced.

(enter JANE)

JANE: Guess what! I've been invited to Mr. Bingley's house for a visit!

BENNET SISTERS: Ooooooo! He likes youuuuuuuuu!

MRS. BENNET: Better go on horseback, because it seems likely to rain; and then you must stay all night.

ELIZABETH: *(sarcastically)* Really? Solid plan, Mom.

JANE: Okay, bye! *(she exits)*

MARY: Hey, look, it's raining!

MRS. BENNET: Woot! My plan is working! *(starts dancing around in a victory dance; ALL exit)*

(enter JANE, MR. BINGLEY, CAROLINE, MR. DARCY, and ELIZABETH; JANE lies on the floor upstage; MR. DARCY is ignoring everyone while reading a book; ELIZABETH enters opposite the rest)

ELIZABETH: Howdy. I'm just here to check on Jane since she got sick from the rain. Hey, that rhymed!

MR. BINGLEY: Welcome! I'm so sorry she got sick. *(JANE coughs in the background)*

CAROLINE: Come walk with me. *(holds out her arm to ELIZABETH)*

ELIZABETH: Um, walk where, Caroline?

CAROLINE: You know, take a turn about the room. *(to audience)* This is what people did before television.

(CAROLINE and ELIZABETH walk in a large circle around MR. BINGLEY and MR. DARCY)

MR. DARCY: You girls are either walking because you have secret affairs to discuss, or because you want to be admired.

MR. BINGLEY: I think they look nice. *(calls over to JANE)* How ya doing, Jane?

(JANE, still lying on the floor, gives two thumbs up and coughs some more)

CAROLINE: *(to ELIZABETH)* What do you think of our Mr. Darcy?

ELIZABETH: Are we talking strengths or weaknesses? Because he doesn't seem like a warm, fuzzy, or forgiving person.

MR. DARCY: My good opinion once lost, is lost forever.

ELIZABETH: *(to CAROLINE)* See? *(to MR. DARCY)* So your defect is to hate everybody.

MR. DARCY: And yours is to willfully misunderstand them. *(JANE moans)*

ELIZABETH: Whatever. I really don't have time for this. Peace out. *(she walks over to JANE and drags her offstage)*

(ALL exit)

(enter ALL BENNETS and MR. COLLINS)

MR. BENNET: Girls, meet my cousin, Mr. Collins, who, when I am dead, may turn you all out of this house as soon as he pleases.

MARY: Wait a minute. Just because we're GIRLS, we can't inherit the house or property?

KITTY: That's sooooo dumb. *(to audience)* No wonder we're all so focused on getting married.

MR. COLLINS: Stinks to be you. Don't worry; I'll take good care of this house someday.

JANE: Let's go to town. You know, get some fresh air. *(MR. and MRS. BENNET exit; ALL others begin walking around the stage in large circle; enter MR. WICKHAM)*

LYDIA: An officer! An officer!

ELIZABETH: *(to MR. WICKHAM)* Hi!

WICKHAM: Hello, ladies! My name is Wickham. I am very handsome and very charming. So you should TOTALLY believe everything I say. *(strikes a pose)*

ELIZABETH: Makes sense.

BENNET SISTERS (EXCEPT ELIZABETH): *(to audience, using "jazz hands")* Foreshadowing!

(enter MR. DARCY and MR. BINGLEY on hobby horses, trotting towards the group onstage)

MR. BINGLEY: Hi Everybody! Helllloooo Jane! *(ALL characters wave back at the men)*

(MR. DARCY stops in front of MR. WICKHAM. He looks disgusted)

MR. DARCY: *(to MR. WICKHAM)* Ugh.

WICKHAM: Ugh to you too. *(sticks out tongue at MR. DARCY and makes spitting noises; MR. DARCY does the same to WICKHAM; MR. BINGLEY and MR. DARCY "ride" offstage)*

ELIZABETH: Um, what was that about?

(MR. WICKHAM takes ELIZABETH's arm and leads her away from the other characters. ALL others whisper amongst themselves)

WICKHAM: Let me tell you my super sad story. That guy on the horse, Mr. Darcy? Well, his dad was my godfather and was going to give me some money so I could be a minister. Then when his dad died, Mr. Darcy didn't give me any money! And I was forced to be a soldier! And Mr. Darcy hates me! *(starts crying melodramatically)*

ELIZABETH: This is quite shocking! He deserves to be publically disgraced! I had not thought Mr. Darcy so bad as this...though I have never liked him.

MR. COLLINS: This town smells like horse poop. Let's leave.

ELIZABETH: *(to MR. WICKHAM)* Gotta go. See ya.

WICKHAM: See ya. *(he bows extravagantly)*

(ALL exit)

(enter ELIZABETH)

ELIZABETH: *(to audience)* You'll never guess where we are now. That's right. Another dance! I was hoping that cute Mr. Wickham would be here, but no luck. I've had to dance with my boring cousin, Mr. Collins, and that terrible Mr. Darcy. *(MR. COLLINS and MR. DARCY enter from opposite sides of the stage and strike dance poses)* Meanwhile, my sister Jane and Mr. Bingley seem happily in love. *(enter JANE and MR. BINGLEY, who begin dancing together, looking happy; enter CAROLINE BINGLEY)*

CAROLINE: *(to ELIZABETH)* So, I hear you are quite delighted with George Wickham! WELL, let me just tell you, as a friend, that you totally shouldn't believe him. I don't know what he told you, but I'm here to tell you, that Mr. Darcy has always been remarkably kind to him.

ELIZABETH: Whatever. Believe what you want, but I believe Mr. Wickham. He's just sooooo charming.

CAROLINE: Whatever. Only trying to help. *(she flips her hair as she exits)*

(MR. COLLINS walks over to ELIZABETH; MR. DARCY, JANE, and MR. BINGLEY exit)

MR. COLLINS: So, Elizabeth, I've decided I need a wife. As soon as I saw you, I singled you out as the companion of my future life. Let's get married!

ELIZABETH: What? No way!

(enter MRS. BENNET, running)

MRS. BENNET: Whaaaaaaaat?? Lizzy, you marry him right now!

ELIZABETH: Um, yeah. Not happening, mom.

MRS. BENNET: *(calls offstage)* Mr. Bennet!! *(enter MR. BENNET)* Make Elizabeth marry Mr. Collins!

MR. BENNET: *(looks at MR. COLLINS, then ELIZABETH, then MRS. BENNET; sighs loudly)* Elizabeth, from this day you must be a stranger to one of your parents. Your mother will never see you again if you do NOT marry Mr. Collins, and I will never see you again if you DO.

MRS. BENNET: Whaaaaaaaat? But...

ELIZABETH: Thanks for having my back, Dad! *(to MR. COLLINS and MRS. BENNET)* Can we forget this whole conversation now?

(enter CHARLOTTE LUCAS)

CHARLOTTE: *(to ELIZABETH)* Hey there, my best friend!!

ELIZABETH: Hey Charlotte!

MR. COLLINS: *(interrupting)* Charlotte...you look like you have...uhhhh...a nice personality.

CHARLOTTE: Thanks!

MR. COLLINS: *(pushes ELIZABETH behind him)* Will YOU marry me?

CHARLOTTE: *(to audience)* He's neither sensible, nor agreeable, but... *(to MR. COLLINS)* Sure, why not?

MR. COLLINS: Perfect. *(to the BENNETS)* Later! *(he and CHARLOTTE link arms and exit)*

MRS. BENNET: See, now there's a girl with some sense.

(ALL exit)

ACT 2 SCENE 1

(enter ELIZABETH and JANE; JANE holds a letter)

JANE: They're gone, Lizzy, all gone! Caroline, Mr. Bingley, and Mr. Darcy have left town and they're not coming back.

ELIZABETH: Good riddance.

JANE: How can you say that! I thought Mr. Bingley was going to marry me. But in this letter, Caroline basically says that he's going to marry Mr. Darcy's sister, Georgiana!

ELIZABETH: Look, Jane, Caroline's a brat. She thinks we have no money and sees that her brother is in love with you, and wants him to marry Georgiana. Well, I KNOW he loves you. Don't worry. Be happy.

JANE: No! He will be forgot, and we shall all be as we were before...single!

ELIZABETH: How depressing. But okay, if you say so.

(enter MR. and MRS. GARDINER and all the BENNETS)

MARY: Welcome, Aunt and Uncle Gardiner!

ALL BENNETS: Hi!

MRS. GARDINER: Thanks, Mary! Hi family! Since we're short on time, I'll get right to the point: Jane, you look sad. How about you come back to London with us when we leave? And you, Elizabeth, I've gotta warn you about that officer, Mr. Wickham. You must not let your fancy run away with you. He doesn't have any money, so you really can't marry him.

MR. GARDINER: Well said, dear. Okay, bye! *(MR. and MRS. GARDINER exit with JANE; all BENNETS except ELIZABETH exit opposite side of stage)*

ELIZABETH: *(to audience)* At present, I am not in love with Mr. Wickham. But he is, beyond all comparison, the most agreeable man I ever saw. *(she sighs; KITTY runs onstage and whispers in ELIZABETH'S ear, then runs offstage)* Oh. Well, apparently Mr. Wickham likes someone else now. Some rich girl. I guess handsome young men must have something to live on as well as the plain. You know, I should really go visit Charlotte and see if she likes being married to Mr. Collins.

ACT 2 SCENE 2

(ELIZABETH starts walking around the stage. Enter CHARLOTTE, MR. COLLINS, and LADY CATHERINE de BOURGH)

CHARLOTTE: You came! I'm a wife now!

MR. COLLINS: Elizabeth, this is Lady Catherine de Bourgh, my patroness.

ELIZABETH: *(to audience)* That's like, his boss. *(to LADY de BOURGH)* Nice to meet you!

LADY de BOURGH: Do you play and sing, Miss Bennet? Do you draw? Has your governess left you?

ELIZABETH: What is this, the Spanish Inquisition? Okay. I sing, I don't draw, and I never had a governess.

LADY de BOURGH: How disappointing. Your mother obviously failed you. I'm going to leave now. *(she exits)*

ELIZABETH: *(sarcastic)* She's pleasant.

(enter MR. DARCY; CHARLOTTE and MR. COLLINS tiptoe offstage)

ELIZABETH: What are YOU doing here?

MR. DARCY: Lady de Bourgh is my aunt. What are YOU doing here?

ELIZABETH: Visiting my best friend. *(motions to where CHARLOTTE was standing and notices that she is now gone)*

MR. DARCY: *(to audience)* Okay. I'm going to skip ahead now because we can't possibly fit every conversation Jane Austen wrote into this play. So Elizabeth and I keep running into each other and each time I realize more and more how smart and amazing she is...

ELIZABETH: *(taps MR. DARCY on the shoulder)* Um, hello?

MR. DARCY: *(takes a deep breath)* In vain I have struggled. It will not do. My feelings will not be repressed. You must allow me to tell you how ardently I admire and love you. Will you marry me?

ELIZABETH: Are you kidding me?

MR. DARCY: Is that a yes?

ELIZABETH: Look. I know you didn't want Mr. Bingley to marry my sister, Jane, because we're poor and my mom's kind of annoying. And I know how terrible you were to Mr. Wickham, leaving him with no money. Why would I marry you? I mean, come on.

MR. DARCY: So...is that a yes?

ELIZABETH: You are the last man in the world whom I could ever be prevailed on to marry. So...no!

MR. DARCY: Fine. *(throws a letter at her)* Read this when you're ready. *(he exits)*

(ELIZABETH picks letter up off floor, rolls her eyes at the audience, and exits)

(enter ELIZABETH)

ELIZABETH: *(to audience)* So, of course, I read his letter. He said that he DID give money to Mr. Wickham after his dad died, but Mr. Wickham spent all the money and then tried to elope with Mr. Darcy's younger sister, Georgiana, in order to get his hands on her money! Say whaaaaaat? And I thought Mr. Wickham was such a gentleman! I was SO wrong! He's kind of a creep!

(enter JANE, LYDIA, KITTY, and MARY)

KITTY: Welcome home! Guess what! We heard that the officers will be encamped near Brighton this summer.

LYDIA: We want Dad to take us there! Because... officers!

ELIZABETH: Seriously, girls? Can you talk about anything else?

LYDIA: Well what about you and Jane? Have you seen any pleasant men? Have you had any flirting? I mean, you both are going to be old maids soon. *(to ELIZABETH)* What, you're about 20 now, right?

JANE: You're so sweet, Lydia.

(enter MR. BENNET)

MR. BENNET: Lydia, the wife of some colonel has invited you to Brighton for the summer, so I guess you can go. *(to audience)* Hopefully, that colonel will keep her out of any real mischief.

JANE, ELIZABETH, & KITTY: *(to audience)* Foreshadowing! *(jazz hands)*

KITTY: Not fair! I want to go, too!

LYDIA: Too bad, so sad. See ya! *(she exits)*

KITTY: Hello, Aunt and Uncle Gardiner!

(enter MR. and MRS. GARDINER)

MRS. GARDINER: *(to ELIZABETH)* Hello! Wanna go with us to take a tour of the English countryside?

MR. GARDINER: *(to audience)* Basically, we just show up to take our nieces places. It's what we're good at.

ELIZABETH: Sure. Let's go in pursuit of novelty and amusement!

(ALL exit)

ACT 2 SCENE 4

(enter ELIZABETH, MRS. GARDINER, and MR. GARDINER)

ELIZABETH: *(looks around)* Wow, the countryside is great!

MRS. GARDINER: Hey, look! *(points across stage)* That's Pemberley! We should go check it out.

MR. GARDINER: Yeah! Looking at mansions is a great way to feel insignificant!

ELIZABETH: *(to audience)* Pemberley is the name of the mansion. Because, of course, big houses deserve fancy sounding names. Also, this particular house belongs to Mr. Darcy. So let's hope he's not home!

(they walk across the stage)

ALL: *(looking at the "house")* Oooooo! Ahhhhhh.

(enter MR. DARCY, MR. BINGLEY, and CAROLINE)

MR. DARCY: What are you doing here?

ELIZABETH: What are YOU doing here?

MR. DARCY: Ummm, this is my house.

ELIZABETH: Makes sense. *(to MR. BINGLEY and CAROLINE)* Long time no see.

MR. BINGLEY: How's your sister, Jane?

ELIZABETH: She's... *(enter JANE)* here?!

JANE: *(to audience)* Shhhhhhh. I'm not really here. *(to ELIZABETH)* At this part in the story, I've sent you a bunch of letters, and well, here they are! *(hands ELIZABETH letters and runs offstage; ELIZABETH, MR. GARDINER, and MRS. GARDINER walk to a corner of the stage and start reading the letters)*

CAROLINE: *(to MR. DARCY, pointing to ELIZABETH)* For my own part, I must confess I never could see any beauty in her.

MR. DARCY: Well I think she is one of the handsomest women of my acquaintance!

ELIZABETH: *(gasps)* OH NO! My sister Lydia has run off with Mr. Wickham! This is terrible! We have to go home right now!

MR. DARCY: That two-faced villain! Yes, you should hurry home now!

(ALL exit)

(enter ALL BENNETS, except LYDIA and MR. BENNET; they are all weeping and wailing)

MRS. BENNET: Poor dear child! And now here's Mr. Bennet gone away to look for her, and I know he will fight Wickham, and then he will be killed!

ELIZABETH: That might be a tad dramatic, Mom.

(enter MR. BENNET, running)

MR. BENNET: I couldn't find her. *(MRS. BENNET cries loudly; enter MR. GARDINER, running)*

MR. GARDINER: *(huffing and puffing as though he has run a long ways)* We found Lydia and Wickham. Here's the deal. Wickham says he'll marry her IF you pay him some money every year.

MRS. BENNET: He HAS to marry her or her honor will be ruined forever!

MR. BENNET: *(pause; MRS. BENNET nudges him)* I don't like it, but okay, deal!

MR. GARDINER: Cool. *(he runs offstage; LYDIA and MR. WICKHAM run onstage)*

LYDIA: I am a married woman! What about my sisters? *(to MRS. BENNET)* They must all go to Brighton. That is the place to get husbands. *(she and MR. WICKHAM laugh)*

ELIZABETH: Um, yeah, no thanks. I do not particularly like your way of getting husbands.

LYDIA: Oh, and let me tell you about the wedding! Let's see. Our aunt and uncle were there, and Mr. Darcy, and... *(MR. WICKHAM covers LYDIA'S mouth to keep her from talking)*

WICKHAM: Okay, that's enough. We should probably leave and get on with our life together.

LYDIA: You're SO right! Bye, family! *(LYDIA and MR. WICKHAM exit)*

ELIZABETH: *(to audience)* Wait. Mr. Darcy was at their wedding?!

(enter MRS. GARDINER)

MRS. GARDINER: *(to ELIZABETH)* Lizzy, Mr. Darcy is the one who found them! And he gave Wickham a bunch of money to marry Lydia. But he didn't want you to know. I think he really, really likes you. Well, that's all I came to say. Bye! *(she exits)*

(enter MR. DARCY and MR. BINGLEY)

MR. BINGLEY: Jane! *(JANE steps forward)* I love you! And, um, I want to marry you!

JANE: Tis too much! I do not deserve it! I'm soooooo happy! *(JANE and MR. BINGLEY start dancing together around the stage)*

MRS. BENNET: Two girls down, three to go! *(ALL exit except ELIZABETH)*

ELIZABETH: *(to audience)* I am kinda jealous. And...I think that I actually love Mr. Darcy! Argh!

(enter MR. DARCY)

MR. DARCY: Hey.

ELIZABETH: Hey.

ELIZABETH and MR. DARCY: So I... *(talking over each other)*

MR. DARCY: *(clears throat)* If your feelings are still what they were last April, tell me so at once. MY affections and wishes are unchanged, but one word from you will silence me on this subject for ever.

ELIZABETH: So you still want to get married?

MR. DARCY: YES!

ELIZABETH: Me too! *(they high-five)*

(enter MR. BENNET, MRS. BENNET, JANE, KITTY, and MARY)

MR. BENNET: *(to ELIZABETH)* Wait! Are you out of your senses? I thought you hated him?

JANE: Oh Lizzy, it cannot be! What is actually happening right now? I'm so confused.

ELIZABETH: *(Big deep breath)* I was wrong. He's actually... a good person. *(THE BENNETS all gasp and whisper amongst themselves)*

MR. DARCY: Yes. We were both prideful...and prejudiced.

MR. BENNET: Well then, congratulations!

MRS. BENNET: You'll be so rich!

ELIZABETH: *(to MRS. BENNET)* I think you mean happy, right?

MRS. BENNET: Ummm sure, that's what I meant.

MR. DARCY: I'm sure that's what she meant.

KITTY: Okay, family, we've got some weddings to plan. Let's DO this! *(ALL exit)*

THE END

SPECIAL THANKS

As with all books that I write, it takes a team. When I first starting writing these books, it was just me and a dream. Now, I have many different individuals that are willing to help out in the creative process and I wanted to send them a little love.

To all of our script reviewers: Suzy Newman, Angi, Eli, Debba, Holli, Bradley, Jean, and Ginger & her boys thank you so very much! This book would not be what it is without you!!!

To my newest illustrator, Ryan Gottlieb. Thanks for your beautiful work. I can't wait to do more projects with you in the future as well as see how you blossom in this career that is so obviously suited for you!

To Adam Watson, for once again creating another author in our collection of author art.

And lastly, a big thanks to Ron Leishman for his creation of Elizabeth and Mr. Darcy. As always, you are spot on in your art. I love seeing your work every day come into my email! You are truly gifted!

The Jungle Book for Kids

PARENT WOLF: Oh hi, Bagheera. What's happening in the life of a panther?

BAGHEERA: I wanted to warn you. Shere Khan's in town again.

PARENT WOLF: The tiger? What's he doing in this part of the jungle?

BAGHEERA: What tigers do. You know, hunt, eat, hunt again, eat... hunt....eat... *(trailing off)*

PARENT WOLF: *(play-acting like a tiger)* Oh look at me, I'm a mean ol' tiger, roar!!! *(there is a LOUD ROAR and GROWL from offstage, PARENT WOLF is a bit shocked)*

BAGHEERA: Listen! That's him now!

(enter MOWGLI, running off-balance, and falling down)

PARENT WOLF: Whoa! A man's cub! Look! *(all turn to look at MOWGLI)* How little and so... smelly, but cute! *(starts petting his hair)*

(BAGHEERA sneaks over to MOWGLI and whispers something in his ear. MOWGLI sighs and gets down on his knees to appear smaller; he remains on his knees throughout the rest of the scene and ACT1 SCENE 2)

MOWGLI: *(very sarcastically)* Gaa gaa. Goo goo.

(SHERE KHAN enters. PARENT WOLF hides MOWGLI behind her back)

SHERE KHAN: A man's cub went this way. Its parents have run off. Give it to me. I'll uh.... take care of him... *(as he rubs his belly)* you can TOTALLY trust me! *(gives* *the audience a big evil smile)*

PARENT WOLF: You are NOT the boss of us.

SHERE KHAN: Excuse me?! Do you know who I am? It is I, Shere Khan, who speaks! I'm kind of a big deal. And scary! GRRRRR.

PARENT WOLF: The man's cub is mine; he shall not be killed! So beat it; you don't scare us.

SHERE KHAN: Fine. But I'll get him some day, make no mistake! Muahahahahaha! ROAR! *(SHERE KHAN exits)*

PARENT WOLF: *(to MOWGLI)* Mowgli the Frog I will call thee. Lie still, little frog.

MOWGLI: *(to PARENT WOLF)* Frog?

PARENT WOLF: *(to MOWGLI and audience)* Yeah, I guess Rudyard Kipling liked frogs! But now we have to see what the wolf leader says.

(enter AKELA, BAGHEERA, and BALOO)

AKELA: Okay, wolves, let's get this meeting started! Howl!

WOLVES: Howl!!! *(all WOLVES howl)*

PARENT WOLF: Akela, our great leader, I'd like to present the newest member of our pack, Mowgli the Frog!

AKELA: Hmmm, Frog, huh? If you say so.

(enter SHERE KHAN)

SHERE KHAN: ROAR! The cub is mine! Give him to me!

AKELA: Who speaks for this cub?

BALOO: *(speaking in a big, deep bear voice!)* I, Baloo the Bear, I speak for the man's cub. I myself will teach him the ways of the jungle.

Hamlet for Kids

(enter GERTRUDE and POLONIUS)

GERTRUDE: What's up, Polonius?

POLONIUS: I am going to hide and spy on your conversation with Hamlet!

GERTRUDE: Oh, okay.

(POLONIUS hides somewhere, enter HAMLET very mad, swinging his sword around)

HAMLET: MOM!!! I AM VERY MAD!

GERTRUDE: Ahhh! You scared me!

(POLONIUS sneezes from hiding spot)

HAMLET: *(not seeing POLONIUS)* How now, a rat? Who's hiding? *(stabs POLONIUS)*

POLONIUS: O, I am slain! Ohhhh the pain! *(dies on stage)*

GERTRUDE: Oh me, what has thou done?

HAMLET: Oops, I thought that was Claudius. Hmph, oh well... as I was saying, I AM MAD you married uncle Claudius!

GERTRUDE: Oh that, yeah, sorry. *(in a motherly voice)* Now, you just killed Polonius, clean up this mess and go to your room!

HAMLET: Okay Mom.

(all exit, HAMLET drags POLONIUS' body off stage)

ACT 4 SCENES 1-3

(enter GERTRUDE and CLAUDIUS)

GERTRUDE: Ahhh, Dear?

CLAUDIUS: Yeah?

GERTRUDE: Ummmm, you would not believe what I have seen tonight! Polonius is dead.

CLAUDIUS: WHAT!?

GERTRUDE: Yeah, Hamlet was acting a little crazy, Polonius sneezed or something, then Hamlet yelled, "A rat, a rat!" and then WHACK! It was over.

CLAUDIUS: *(very angry)* HAMLET!!!! GET OVER HERE NOW!!!!!

(enter HAMLET)

CLAUDIUS: *(very casual)* Hey, what's up?

HAMLET: What noise, who calls on Hamlet? What do you want?

CLAUDIUS: Now, Hamlet. Where's Polonius' body?

HAMLET: I'm not telling!

CLAUDIUS: Oh come on, please tell me!!! Please! With a cherry on top! Where is Polonius?

HAMLET: Oh, all right. He's over there, up the stairs into the lobby. *(points off stage)*

(POLONIUS enters and dies again)

CLAUDIUS: Ewe... he's a mess! Hamlet, I am sending you off to England.

HAMLET: Fine! Farewell, dear Mother. And I'm taking this with me! *(HAMLET grabs POLONIUS and drags him off stage)*

(all exit but CLAUDIUS)

CLAUDIUS: *(to audience)* I have arranged his execution in England! *(laughs evilly as he exits)* Muwahahaha....

The Tempest for Kids

PROSPERO: Hast thou, spirit, performed to point the tempest that I bade thee?

ARIEL: What? Was that English?

PROSPERO: *(Frustrated)* Did you make the storm hit the ship?

ARIEL: Why didn't you say that in the first place? Oh yeah! I rocked that ship! They didn't know what hit them.

PROSPERO: Why, that's my spirit! But are they, Ariel, safe?

ARIEL: Not a hair perished.

PROSPERO: Woo-hoo! All right. We've got more work to do.

ARIEL: Wait a minute. You're still going to free me, right, Master?

PROSPERO: Oh, I see. Is it sooooo terrible working for me? Huh? Remember when I saved you from that witch? Do you? Remember when that blue-eyed hag locked you up and left you for dead? Who saved you? Me, that's who!

ARIEL: I thank thee, master.

PROSPERO: I will free you in two days, okay? Sheesh. Patience is a virtue, or haven't you heard. Right. Where was I? Oh yeah... I need you to disguise yourself like a sea nymph and then... *(PROSPERO whispers something in ARIEL'S ear)* Got it?

ARIEL: Got it. *(ARIEL exits)*

PROSPERO: *(to MIRANDA)* Awake, dear heart, awake!

(MIRANDA yawns loudly)

PROSPERO: Shake it off. Come on. We'll visit Caliban, my slave.

MIRANDA: The witch's son? You mean the MONSTER! He's creepy and stinky!!!

PROSPERO: Mysterious and sneaky,

MIRANDA: Altogether freaky,

MIRANDA & PROSPERO: He's Caliban the slave!!! *(snap, snap!)*

PROSPERO: *(Calls offstage)* What, ho! Slave! Caliban!

(enter CALIBAN)

CALIBAN: Oh, look it's the island stealers! This is my home! My mother, the witch, left it to me and now you treat me like dirt.

MIRANDA: Oh boo-hoo! I used to feel sorry for you, I even taught you our language, but you tried to hurt me so now we have to lock you in that cave.

CALIBAN: I wish I had never learned your language!

PROSPERO: Go get us wood! If you don't, I'll rack thee with old cramps, and fill all thy bones with aches!

CALIBAN: *(to AUDIENCE)* He's so mean to me! But I have to do what he says. ANNOYING! *(exit CALIBAN)*

(enter FERDINAND led by "invisible" ARIEL)

ARIEL: *(Singing)* Who let the dogs out?! Woof, woof, woof!! *(Spookily)* The watchdogs bark; bow-wow, bow-wow!

FERDINAND: *(Dancing across stage)* Where should this music be? Where is it taking me! What's going on?

Two Gentlemen of Verona for Kids

ANTONIO: It's not nothing.

PROTEUS: Ahhhhh......It's a letter from Valentine, telling me what a great time he's having in Milan, yeah... that's what it says!

ANTONIO: Awesome! Glad to hear it! Because, you leave tomorrow to join Valentine in Milan.

PROTEUS: What!? Dad! No way! I don't want... I mean, I need some time. I've got some things to do.

ANTONIO: Like what?

PROTEUS: You know...things! Important things! And stuff! Lots of stuff!

ANTONIO: No more excuses! Go pack your bag. *(ANTONIO begins to exit)*

PROTEUS: Fie!

ANTONIO: What was that?

PROTEUS: Fiiii......ne with me, Pops! *(ANTONIO exits)* I was afraid to show my father Julia's letter, lest he should take exceptions to my love; and my own lie of an excuse made it easier for him to send me away.

ANTONIO: *(Offstage)* Proteus! Get a move on!!

PROTEUS: Fie!!!

(exit)

ACT 2 SCENE 1

(enter VALENTINE and SPEED following)

VALENTINE: Ah, Silvia, Silvia! *(heavy sighs)*

SPEED: *(mocking)* Madam Silvia! Madam Silvia! Gag me.

VALENTINE: Knock it off! You don't know her.

SPEED: Do too. She's the one that you can't stop staring at. Makes me wanna barf.

VALENTINE: I do not stare!

SPEED: You do. AND you keep singing that silly love song. *(sing INSERT SAPPY LOVE SONG)* You used to be so much fun.

VALENTINE: Huh? *(heavy sigh, starts humming SAME LOVE SONG)*

SPEED: Never mind.

VALENTINE: I have loved her ever since I saw her. Here she comes!

SPEED: Great. *(to audience)* Watch him turn into a fool.

(enter SILVIA)

VALENTINE: Hey, Silvia.

SILVIA: Hey, Valentine. What's goin' on?

VALENTINE: Nothin'. What's goin' on with you?

SILVIA: Nothin'.

(pause)

VALENTINE: What are you doing later?

SILVIA: Not sure. Prob-ly nothin'. You?

VALENTINE: Me neither. Nothin'.

SILVIA: Yea?

VALENTINE: Probably.

SPEED: *(to audience)* Kill me now.

SILVIA: Well, I guess I better go.

VALENTINE: Oh, okay! See ya'..

(pause)

SILVIA: See ya' later maybe?

VALENTINE: Oh, yea! Maybe! Yea! Okay!

SILVIA: Bye.

VALENTINE: Bye!

(exit SILVIA)

SPEED: *(aside)* Wow. *(to VALENTINE)* Dude, what the heck was that?

VALENTINE: I think she has a boyfriend. I can tell.

SPEED: Dude! She is so into you! How could you not see that?

VALENTINE: Do you think?

SPEED: Come on. We'll talk it through over dinner. *(to audience)* Fool. Am I right?

(exit)

The Three Musketeers
for Kids

(ATHOS and D'ARTAGNAN enter)

ATHOS: Glad you could make it. I have engaged two of my friends as seconds.

D'ARTAGNAN: Seconds?

ATHOS: Yeah, they make sure we fight fair. Oh, here they are now!

(enter ARAMIS and PORTHOS singing, "Bad boys, bad boys, watcha gonna do...")

PORTHOS: Hey! I'm fighting him in an hour. I am going to fight... because...well... I am going to fight!

ARAMIS: And I fight him at two o'clock! Ours is a theological quarrel. *(does a thinking pose)*

D'ARTAGNAN: Yeah, yeah, yeah.... I'll get to you soon!

ATHOS: We are the Three Musketeers; Athos, Porthos, and Aramis.

D'ARTAGNAN: Whatever, Ethos, Pathos, and Logos, let's just finish this! *(swords crossed and are about to fight; enter JUSSAC and cardinal's guards)*

PORTHOS: The cardinal's guards! Sheathe your swords, gentlemen.

JUSSAC: Dueling is illegal! You are under arrest!

ARAMIS: *(to ATHOS and PORTHOS)* There are five of them and we are but three.

D'ARTAGNAN: *(steps forward to join them)* It appears to me we are four! I have the spirit; my heart is that of a Musketeer.

PORTHOS: Great! I love fighting!

(Musketeers say "Fight, fight fight!...Fight, fight, fight!" as they are fighting; D'ARTAGNAN fights JUSSAC and it's the big fight; JUSSAC is wounded and exits; the 3 MUSKETEERS cheer)

ATHOS: Well done! Let's go see Treville and the king!

ARAMIS: And we don't have to kill you now!

PORTHOS: And let's get some food, too! I'm hungry!

D'ARTAGNAN: *(to audience)* This is fun!

(ALL exit)

ACT 2 SCENE 1

(enter 3 MUSKETEERS, D'ARTAGNAN, and TREVILLE)

TREVILLE: The king wants to see you, and he's not too happy you killed a few of the cardinal's guards.

(enter KING)

KING: *(yelling)* YOU GUYS HUMILIATED THE CARDINAL'S GUARDS!

ATHOS: Sire, they attacked us!

KING: Oh...Well then, bravo! I hear D'Artagnan beat the cardinal's best swordsman! Brave young man! Here's some money for you. Enjoy! *(hands money to D'ARTAGNAN)*

D'ARTAGNAN: Sweet!

(ALL exit)

Richard III for Kids

ACT 1 SCENE 4

(CLARENCE is in prison, sleeping. He wakes up from a bad dream)

CLARENCE: Terrible, horrible, no good, very bad dream! *(pauses, notices audience and addresses them)* O, I have pass'd a miserable night! I dreamt that Richard was trying to kill me! Hahahaha, Richard is SUCH a good guy, he would NEVER do a thing like that!

(Enter MURDERER carrying a weapon)

MURDERER: I sounded like such a pro, no one will know it's my first day on the job! Hehehe!

CLARENCE: Hey! Who's there?

MURDERER: Um... um.... *(hides his murder weapon behind his back)*

CLARENCE: Your eyes do menace me. Are you planning to murder me? 'Cause that's not a good idea. My brother Richard is a REALLY powerful guy.

MURDERER: Ha! Richard is the one who sent me here to do this! *(a pause)* Whoops...

CLARENCE: Hahaha, you foolish fellow. Richard loves me.

MURDERER: Dude, what are you not getting? He PAID me to do this!

CLARENCE: O, do not slander him, for he is kind.

(The MURDERER stabs CLARENCE. CLARENCE dies a dramatic death)

CLARENCE: Kinda ruthless... *(dies)*

MURDERER: *(Gasps)* Oh, my! He's dead! I feel bad now.... I bet Clarence was a really nice guy. Ahhh, the guilt! Wow, I should have stayed in clown school.

(MURDERER exits)

ACT 2 SCENE 1

(KING EDWARD is surrounded by QUEEN ELIZABETH and BUCKINGHAM)

KING EDWARD: Well, this has been a great day at work! Everyone's agreed to get along!

(ELIZABETH and BUCKINGHAM shake hands with each other to celebrate the peace. Enter RICHARD. KING EDWARD smiles happily)

KING EDWARD: If I die, I will be at peace! But I must say I'm feeling a lot healthier after all of this peace-making!

RICHARD: Hey! Looks like you're all in a good mood. That's great, 'cause you know I LOVE getting along! So what's up?

KING EDWARD: I made them like each other!

RICHARD: How lovely! I like you all now, too! Group hug? *(everyone shakes their head)* No? *(he grins sweetly)*

ELIZABETH: Wonderful! Once Clarence gets back from the Tower, everything will be perfect!

RICHARD: WHAT??? We make peace and then you insult us like this? That's no way to talk about a DEAD man!!

(EVERYONE gasps)

KING EDWARD: Is Clarence dead? I told them to cancel the execution!

RICHARD: Oh, yeah... guess that was too late! *(winks to audience)*

KING EDWARD: Nooooooo!!!! Oh my poor brother! Now I feel more sick than EVER! Oh, poor Clarence!

(All exit except RICHARD and BUCKINGHAM)

RICHARD: Well, that sure worked as planned!

BUCKINGHAM: Great job, partner!

(both exit, laughing evilly)

Macbeth for Kids

ACT 2 SCENE 1

(DUNCAN runs on stage and dies with a dagger stuck in him, MACBETH drags his body off and then returns with the bloody dagger. LADY MACBETH enters)

LADY MACBETH: Did you do it?

MACBETH: *(clueless)* Do what?

LADY MACBETH: KILL HIM!

MACBETH: Oh yeah, all done. I have done the deed.

LADY MACBETH: *(pointing at the dagger)* What is that?

MACBETH: What?

LADY MACBETH: Why do you still have the bloody dagger with you?

MACBETH: Ummmmm, I don't know.

LADY MACBETH: Well go put it back!

MACBETH: NO! I'll go no more! I'm scared of the dark, and there is a dead body in there. I am afraid to think what I have done.

LADY MACBETH: Man you are a wimp, give me the dagger. *(LADY MACBETH takes the dagger, exits, and returns)*

LADY MACBETH: All done.

(there is a loud knock at the door)

LADY MACBETH: It's 2am! This really is not a good time for more visitors. *(goes to the door)* Who is it? *(opens door)*

MACDUFF: It is Macduff. I am here to see the king.

MACBETH: He is sleeping in there.

(MACDUFF exits while MACBETH and LADY MACBETH look at each other)

MACDUFF: *(off stage scream)* AGHHHHHHHHHHH – He's dead, he's dead!!! *(MACDUFF enters)*

MACBETH: Who?

MACDUFF: Who do you think? *(they both scream)*

BANQUO: *(BANQUO, MALCOLM, and DONALBAIN enter)* What happened, can't someone get a good night sleep around here?

MACDUFF: The king has been murdered.

MALCOLM & DONALBAIN: Aghhhhhhhh!!!!!!!!

DONALBAIN: We must be next.

MALCOLM: Let's get out of here.

DONALBAIN: I'm heading to Ireland.

MALCOLM: I'm off to England. *(MALCOLM and DONALBAIN exit)*

MACDUFF: Well, since there is no one left to be King, why don't you do it Mac?

LADY MACBETH & MACBETH: Okay. *(LADY MACBETH, MACBETH and MACDUFF exit)*

BANQUO: *(to audience)* I fear, thou play'dst most foully for't. *(MACBETH returns)*

MACBETH: Bank, what are you thinking over there?

BANQUO: Oh, nothing. *(said with a big fake smile)* Gotta go! See ya! *(BANQUO exits)*

Sneak peek of

Christmas Carol
for Kids

(enter GHOST PRESENT wearing a robe and holding a turkey leg and a goblet)

GHOST PRESENT: Wake up, Scrooge! I am the Ghost of Christmas Present. Look upon me!

SCROOGE: I'm looking. Not that impressed. But let's get on with it.

GHOST PRESENT: Touch my robe! *(SCROOGE touches GHOST PRESENT's robe. Pause. They look at each other)* Er...it must be broken. Guess we walk. Come on. *(they begin walking downstage)*

SCROOGE: Where are we going?

GHOST PRESENT: Your employee, Bob Cratchit's house. Oh look, here we are.

(enter BOB, MRS. CRATCHIT, MARTHA CRATCHIT, and TINY TIM, who has a crutch in one hand; they are all holding bowls)

BOB: *(to audience)* Hi, we're the Cratchit family. We are a REALLY happy family!

MRS. CRATCHIT: *(to audience)* Yes, but we're REALLY poor, too. Thanks to HIS boss! *(pointing at BOB)*

MARTHA: *(to audience)* Yeah, as you can see our bowls are empty. *(shows empty bowl)* We practically survive off air.

TINY TIM: *(to audience)* But we're happy!

MRS. CRATCHIT: *(to audience; overly sappy)* Because we have each other.

TINY TIM: And love!

SCROOGE: *(to GHOST PRESENT)* Seriously, are they for real?

GHOST PRESENT: Yep! Adorable, isn't it?

BOB: A merry Christmas to us all.

TINY TIM: God bless us every one!

SCROOGE: Spirit, tell me if Tiny Tim will live.

GHOST PRESENT: *(puts hands to head as if looking into the future)* Ooooo, not so good....I see a vacant seat in the poor chimney corner, and a crutch without an owner. If SOMEBODY doesn't change SOMETHING, the child will die.

SCROOGE: No, no! Say he will be spared.

GHOST PRESENT: Nope, can't do that, sorry. Unless SOMEONE decides to change...hint, hint.

BOB: A Christmas toast to my boss, Mr. Scrooge! The founder of the feast!

MRS. CRATCHIT: *(angrily)* Oh sure, Mr. Scrooge! If he were here I'd give him a piece of my mind to feast upon. What an odious, stingy, hard, unfeeling man!

BOB: Dear, it's Christmas day. He's not THAT bad. *(Pause)* He's just... THAT sad. *(BOB holds up his bowl)* Come on, kids, to Scrooge! He probably needs it more than us!

MARTHA & TINY TIM: *(holding up their bowls)* To Scrooge!

MRS. CRATCHIT: *(muttering)* Thanks for nothing.

BOB: That's not nice.

MARTHA: And we Cratchits are ALWAYS nice. Read

the book, Mom.

MRS. CRATCHIT: Sorry.

(the CRATCHIT FAMILY exits)

SCROOGE: She called me odious! Do I really smell that bad?

GHOST PRESENT: Odious doesn't mean you stink. Although in this case you do... According to the dictionary, odious means "unequivocally detestable." I mean, you are a toad sometimes Mr. Scrooge.

SCROOGE: Wow... that's kind of ... mean.

Taming of the Shrew for Kids

ACT 1 SCENE 1

(Enter LUCENTIO and TRANIO)

LUCENTIO: Well, Tranio, my trusty servant, here we are in Padua, Italy! I can't wait to start studying and learn all about philosophy and virtue!

TRANIO: There is such a thing as too much studying, master Lucentio. We need to remember to have fun too! PARTY!

LUCENTIO: Hey look! Here come some of the locals!

(LUCENTIO and TRANIO move to side of stage; Enter BAPTISTA, KATHERINA, BIANCA, HORTENSIO and GREMIO)

BAPTISTA: Look guys, you know the rules: Bianca can't marry anybody until her older sister, Katherina, is married. That's the plan and I'm sticking to it! If either of you both love Katherina, then please, take her.

KATHERINA: *(Sarcastically)* Wow, thanks Dad.

HORTENSIO: I wouldn't marry her if she were the last woman on earth.

KATHERINA: And I'd rather scratch your face off than marry you!

TRANIO: *(Aside to LUCENTIO)* That wench is stark mad!

BAPTISTA: Enough of this! Bianca, go inside.

BIANCA: Yes, dearest father. My books and

instruments shall be my company. *(She exits)*

KATHERINA: *(At BIANCA)* Goody two-shoes.

BAPTISTA: Bianca is so talented in music, instruments, and poetry! I really need to hire some tutors for her. *(KATHERINA rolls her eyes and sighs)* Good-day everyone! *(BAPTISTA exits)*

KATHERINA: *(Very angry)* AGHHHH!!!! I'm outta here

(Exits opposite direction from her father)

GREMIO: *(Shudders)* Ugh! How could anyone ever want to marry Katherina?!

HORTENSIO: I don't know, but let's find a husband for her.

GREMIO: A husband? A devil!

HORTENSIO: I say a husband.

GREMIO: I say a devil.

HORTENSIO: Alright, alright! There's got to be a guy out there crazy enough to marry her.

GREMIO: Let's get to it!

(Exit GREMIO and HORTENSIO)

LUCENTIO: Oh, Tranio! Sweet Bianca, has stolen my heart! I burn, I pine, I perish! Oh, how I love her!

TRANIO: Whoa, Master! You're getting a little over dramatic, there, Lucentio.

LUCENTIO: Sorry. But my heart is seriously on fire! How am I going to make her fall in love with me if she's not allowed to date anybody? Hmmm...

TRANIO: What if you pretended to be a tutor and went to teach her?

LUCENTIO: YOU ARE BRILLIANT, TRANIO! And because we're new here and no one knows what we look like yet, YOU will pretend to be ME at all the local parties. Quick, let's change clothes.

TRANIO: Here? Now?

LUCENTIO: Yes, Here and now! You can't stop this lovin' feeling! *(Starts singing a love song)*

TRANIO: Please, no singing. I'll do it. *(They exchange hats, socks or jackets)*

Oliver Twist
for Kids

(enter FAGIN, SIKES, DODGER and NANCY)

DODGER: So that Oliver kid got caught by the police.

FAGIN: He could tell them all our secrets and get us in trouble; we've got to find him. Like, in the next 30 seconds or so.

SIKES: Send Nancy. She's good at getting information quick.

NANCY: Nope. Don't wanna go, Sikes. I like the kid.

SIKES: She'll go, Fagin.

NANCY: No, she won't, Fagin.

SIKES: Yes, she will, Fagin.

NANCY: Fine! Grrrrr....

(NANCY sticks out her tongue at SIKES and storms offstage, then immediately returns)

NANCY: Okay, I checked with my sources and, some gentleman took him home to take care of him.

(NANCY, DODGER and SIKES stare at FAGIN waiting for direction)

FAGIN: Where?

NANCY: I don't know.

FAGIN: WHAT!?!? *(waiting)* Well don't just stand there, GO FIND HIM! *(to audience)* Can't find any good help these days!

(all run offstage, bumping into each other in their haste)

ACT 2 SCENE 2

(enter OLIVER)

OLIVER: *(to audience)* I'm out running an errand for Mr. Brownlow to prove that I'm a trustworthy boy. I can't keep hanging out with thieves, right?

(enter NANCY, who runs over to OLIVER and grabs him; SIKES, FAGIN, and DODGER enter shortly after and follow NANCY)

NANCY: Oh my dear brother! I've found him! Oh! Oliver! Oliver!

OLIVER: What!?!? I don't have a sister!

NANCY: You do now, kid. Let's go. *(she drags OLIVER to FAGIN)*

FAGIN: Dodger, take Oliver and lock him up.

DODGER: *(to OLIVER)* Sorry, dude. *(DODGER and OLIVER start to exit)*

OLIVER: Aw, man! Seriously? I just found a good home...

NANCY: Don't be too mean to him, Fagin.

OLIVER: *(as he's exiting)* Yeah, don't be too mean to me, Fagin!

SIKES: *(mimicking NANCY)* Don't be mean, Fagin. Wah, wah, wah. Look, I need Oliver to help me rob a house, okay? He is just the size I want to fit through the window. All sneaky ninja like.

Treasure Island
for Kids

(enter JIM, TRELAWNEY, and DOCTOR; enter CAPTAIN SMOLLETT from the other side of the stage)

TRELAWNEY: Hello Captain. Are we all shipshape and seaworthy?

CAPTAIN: Trelawney, I don't know what you're thinking, but I don't like this cruise; and I don't like the men.

TRELAWNEY: *(very angry)* Perhaps you don't like the ship?

CAPTAIN: Nope, I said it short and sweet.

DOCTOR: What? Why?

CAPTAIN: Because I heard we are going on a treasure hunt and the coordinates of the island are: *(whispers to DOCTOR)*

DOCTOR: Wow! That's exactly right!

CAPTAIN: There's been too much blabbing already.

DOCTOR: Right! But, I doubt ANYTHING will go wrong!

CAPTAIN: Fine. Let's sail!

(ALL exit)

Act 2 Scene 3

(enter JIM, SILVER, and various other pirates)

SILVER: Ay, ay, mates. You know the song: Fifteen men on the dead man's chest.

ALL PIRATES: Yo-ho-ho and a bottle of rum!

(PIRATES slowly exit)

JIM: *(to the audience)* So, the Hispaniola had begun her voyage to the Isle of Treasure. As for Long John, well, he still is the nicest cook...

SILVER: Do you want a sandwich?

JIM: That would be great, thanks Long John! *(SILVER exits; JIM addresses audience)* As you can see, Long John is a swell guy! Until....

(JIM hides in the corner)

Act 2 Scene 4

(enter SILVER and OTHER PIRATES)

JIM: *(to audience)* I overheard Long John talking to the rest of the pirates.

SILVER: Listen here you, Scallywags! I was with Captain Flint when he hid this treasure. And those cowards have the map. Follow my directions, and no killing, yet. Clear?

DICK: Clear.

SILVER: But, when we do kill them, I claim Trelawney. And remember, dead men don't bite.

GEORGE: Ay, ay, Long John!

(ALL exit but JIM)

JIM: *(to audience)* Oh no! Long John Silver IS the one-legged man that Billy Bones warned me about! I have to tell the others!

(JIM runs off stage)

ABOUT THE AUTHORS

BRENDAN P. KELSO, came to writing modified Shakespeare scripts when he was taking time off from work to be at home with his newly born son. "It just grew from there". Within months, he was being asked to offer classes in various locations and acting organizations along the Central Coast of California. Originally employed as an engineer, Brendan never thought about writing. However, his unique personality, humor, and love for engaging the kids with The Bard has led him to leave the engineering world and pursue writing as a new adventure in life! He has always believed, "the best way to learn is to have fun!" Brendan makes his home on the Central Coast of California and loves to spend time with his wife and son.

KHARA C. BARNHART first fell in love with Shakespeare in 8th grade after reading Hamlet, and she has been an avid fan ever since. She studied Shakespeare's works in Stratford-upon-Avon, and graduated with a degree in English from UCLA. Khara is lucky to have a terrific career and a charmed life on the Central Coast of CA, but what she cherishes most is time spent with her husband and children. She is delighted to have this chance to help kids foster their own appreciation of Shakespeare in a way that is educational, entertaining, and most importantly, fun!

NOTES